Life Success Series

The Success Within: Be In It to Win It!

BY

Bruce H. Dobbs

 **Publications, Inc.**

Atlanta, Georgia -- USA

The Success Within: Be In It to Win It!

All inquiries should be addressed to:

Dobbs, Bruce H.
Be In It To Win It Publications, Inc.
5372 Lombard Road Ellenwood Ga 30294
The Success Within/Bruce Ellenwood, Georgia 30294
BruceDobbs@BruceDobbs.com
www.brucedobbs.com

Bruce H. Dobbs

Audience: Age 14 and up
Audience: Grades 9 and up

ISBN #: 0-9779217-0-0

Categories:

Success – Psychological
Self-Realization
Self-Help
Wealth
Motivation

Edited by Jacqueline D. Knight
Knight Owl Communications, Tampa, Florida, USA
prjacqui@yahoo.com

Table of Contents

Dedications and Acknowledgements

Dear Friend:

As I look over my life, the people who have impacted my life are too numerous to mention. But, I would like to try in my own small way to say "Thanks" to some very special people.

This book is dedicated to my Father, Howard Dobbs, my mother, Julia Dobbs and my family, Erica, Ashley, Jeff, Andrew, Ananda and Solomon. These are the people who make me the man that I am today.

I would like to acknowledge some very special friends; Toye Kirkland, Greg Baranco, Belinda Pedroso, Roger Bruce, David Martin, Ronald Brown, Don Smart, William Pan, Omar Greene, Sye Gill, Chris Cardell, Mike Boozer, James Jenkins, Steve Young, Maynard Jackson, Osei Adoma, Leon Goodrum, George and Pam Saunders, Jeff and Susan Byrd, Bert Girigori, Donna and Denny Wilmot, Dayle and Donny Burns, Jean and Joan, Carl and Karen, Janet, Lori, Miralda, Julia Lee, Janice, Maudestine and Tommy, Howard and Linda, Shirley and Delmar, The Vismales, Gary Mitchell, Porter Bingham, Sheldon Perry, Kwadna Ashanti, Baby "T", Dennis Hinton Mike Chester and Aleta Gardner for their help, support, friendship and guidance.

And a special "Thank you" to Jacqueline Knight of Knight Owl Communications in Tampa, Florida; my editor, public relations consultant, devoted friend and business associate. I'm sorry if I left anyone out. My editor says that I'm out of space!

A toast to all of you! You are truly a reflection of "My Success Within."

Sincerely,

Bruce H. Dobbs

Preface

WHY CAN'T I JUST DO IT!

"Success is like baking a cake. We all know that simply sitting around and thinking about it doesn't get it done. You've got to follow a recipe that contains a sequence of doable, small, and often, detailed steps in order to produce a quality product."

Bruce Dobbs

Congratulations! You have taken the first, essential step to reaching your goals and dreams.

This book should be used with its companion workbook. If you purchased them as a packaged set, you are on the road to discovering your Success Within! If not, you can simply use a blank sheet of paper to complete the various exercises.

Illustrations have been included to make it easy for you to follow along on this step-by-step map to your outrageous success!

Before you begin packing for your trip to Successville. It is critical that you are aware of baggage you may not want to carry. When I talk about failure; how and why it happens, you will learn to identify some of the most common causes for failing to achieve one's dreams.

You will also get into the meat and potatoes of success. I will give you a clear and distinct roadmap to get you to your goals. You cannot change what has happened to you in the past. You can however, with knowledge of your past, be conscious of the present and create your future.

Introduction

It must be borne in mind that the tragedy of life does not lie in not reaching your goal. The tragedy lies in having no goal to reach. It isn't a calamity to die with dreams unfulfilled, but it is a calamity not to dream. It is a disaster to have no ideal to capture. It is not a disgrace not to reach the stars, but it is a disgrace to have no stars to reach for. Not failure, but low aim is sin.

Benjamin E. Mays

 Imagine that money is no object, and you can do absolutely anything that you want. What would you be doing right now? Do you see yourself running a multi-national corporation? Or better still, are you running a multi-national company from your beach chair outside your second or third home?

Are you taking more time to discover your spiritual side or helping the less fortunate? Are you back in school earning an advanced degree? Are you vacationing with your family, or simply spending much more leisure time? Is what you are dreaming of doing your measure of success?

If success is your destination then your vision, goals and strategies are the vehicle that will get you there. Your determination, willingness to work hard, attitude and personality are the fuel and YOU are the driver. In other words, YOU determine the direction and the speed that will take you to your destination: Success!

If the truth were told, your success is closer than you think. Your success is inside of you. Your success is within you. For many of you, it is merely lying dormant; waiting for the spark that will ignite and send you blasting off towards your dreams.

Someone once said that, "Wisdom is merely knowing what to do next, "and that is why I developed my Success Within strategies.

Many people are not successful because they don't know what to do next. They don't know where they are going and they don't know how to get there. They are wandering through life aimlessly… lost… with no direction. "The Success Within" Series will show you how to get where you decide it is that you want to go.

I developed the Success Within strategies BEFORE I was successful. I realized early on that in order to get where I wanted to go, I would need a roadmap. I saw successful people all around me, but no one ever sat me down and taught me how to be a success. No one ever taught me how to "Be in It to Win It!"

Prior to beginning any trip, you must pack the essential things that you will need to make your journey easier and more comfortable. As you read these pages, you will discover "Success Within" strategies and tools you will need in order to start your trek to "The Success Within" you.

There was a time in my life, when I had to begin at the beginning -- again. For many years, I had lived a seemingly charmed life and achieved many great successes. Then suddenly it was gone. I had somehow managed to let it slip away. From that point, I became determined to not only learn as much as I could about myself, but also about success and money and how to keep them.

Before you can achieve success or "Be In It to Win It," you must first identify and establish exactly what is "The Success Within" you. For this step, planning is a key element.

I began by discovering who I am. I took up a serious study of self-development. I read as much as I could about any topic available on personal growth. I asked myself, "What do I do well and what skills do I need to add or improve?"

 I took an honest self-assessment of my strengths and weaknesses, my talents and my blind spots. From there, I began to define and redefine my core values and my values systems. The answers to those questions that I asked in the first paragraph (What would you be doing right now? Do you see yourself running a multi-national corporation?) are part of your core values system. They tell you what is important to you and what is not. You cannot develop a clear vision until you know and understand your core values.

Your values and beliefs are the ideals that guide or qualify your personal conduct, your interaction with others, and your involvement in your career or business. Like morals, they help you to distinguish between what is right from what is wrong. Your values guide you and help you to conduct your life in a meaningful way.

Values need to be considered when planning your life because they influence your choice of occupation, business, company, corporate culture, work-family balance, social and community involvement.

For instance, if you value good health, you will make time for exercise and proper nutrition. Or, if you value career satisfaction, you will take time to examine your values and make choices that are consistent with them. If you value social involvement you may contribute to your church or community.

We all know, or at least have heard of, someone who has gone to college and received a degree in a particular discipline. Let's just say law. He or she may toil away for years working hard and making a decent, and sometimes, very lucrative living. Then suddenly, and to everyone's surprise, they change course and go off to be a missionary in Africa, start a ministry, open a pet store or launch a singing career.

When you dig deeper, you sometimes discover that the person never really enjoyed the law, hated defending criminals and despised working 17-hour days. Her passion was dancing. He had five dogs and six cats and loved animals. Or she was only truly satisfied when she was singing in the church choir.

He or she chose the profession for the money, or because of a family obligation, or any one of a thousand reasons that had nothing to do with what they really wanted to do with their lives. They probably never explored their core values system to determine what would make them happy, personally satisfied and successful.

Identifying your core values system isn't difficult if you look at the four major categories: (1) Material values; money or something with monetary worth; (2) Personal or Perceived values such as honesty, reliability, and trust are principles that define you as an individual and determine how you will face the world and relate to people; (3) Human/Social or Cultural Values like the practice of your faith or customs that sustain connections with your cultural roots and help you feel connected to a larger community of people with similar backgrounds and; (4) Work Values that determine how you relate to your business or occupation within the social norms.

These are the principles that guide your behavior in professional contexts. These define how you work and how you relate to your employees, co-workers, bosses, and clients. They also reveal your potential for advancement and success.

"The Success Within," will help you explore your inner-self to determine and define the core values that will help you in developing a clear, achievable vision, concrete goals and realistic, workable strategies.

For those of you raising children, it is never too early to help them learn to identify their core values system.

Children should be taught to develop goals and strategies as soon as they are able to read and write. Developing these abilities at a young age will help your child a great deal when they are deciding what they want to do with their education and their lives. In "The Success Within," I offer many self-assessment forms and tests that you can easily translate for children to help teach these vital life skills.

Our goals and objectives are derived from our core values. Our strategies and our personal mission statement are some of the tools we will need on the road to success. All of these tools and skills are outlined in detail in "The Success Within." They will help to develop your "Success Within." You will Be In It to Win It!

Everyday is a Holiday and Every Meal Is a Feast ...

You Have To Be In It To Win It!

Discover your Success Within!

CHAPTER ONE

Mind Games:
Getting the Clarity That Achieves Success

"Take the time to think. Discover your real reason for being here and then have the courage to act on it. The Sages of Sivana all took time daily to silently contemplate not only where they were but also where they were going. They took the time to reflect on their purpose and how they were living their lives every day. Most importantly, they thought deeply and genuinely about how they would improve the next day."

"The Monk Who Sold His Ferrari", by Robin S. Sharma

CHAPTER ONE

Mind Games: Getting the Clarity That Achieves Success

Who's in Charge You or Your Mind?

I have always found it interesting when people who are faced with a new or unfamiliar task say, "my mind just won't let me do this." Upon hearing such a claim, I usually ask them, "Who is in charge -- you or your mind?

The answer to this $64,000 question is simple: **You are in charge!** Your mind will do what you tell it to do. Your mind works for you. You are the boss.

These days, it is in vogue for many people to classify themselves as either left or right-brained dominant. If you subscribe to these labels, you are limiting your ability to develop. By saying, "I cannot do X, or I don't have the mental capacity for Y", you are stifling your ability to be successful.   You are allowing yourself to live out something that is not true.

If you are weak in any skill area, it is only because you have yet to develop skills in that area. You must consider yourself a whole-brained person.

As a child, I somehow got the notion that I was not good in math. I floundered around in math classes until one of my teachers told me that I had a great aptitude for math. I believed her. I began to find math interesting. I improved significantly in my math skills to the point where I began to get A's on the exams. Like your muscles, your mental skills improve with exercise.

When I learn a new form in my Kung fu style Tiger Crane, in the beginning, I am awkward, clumsy, rhythmless and have a difficult time remembering which foot, hand, knee, elbow or finger to move next. It would be embarrassing, except that I know from the experience of learning and mastering other forms that the more you practice the better you get.

Like cutting a path through the forest, the more you travel that path the more defined the path becomes. If you do not travel the path often, weeds bushes and such may grow to obscure the path.

Through the Looking Glass Darkly

A leading impediment to success and happiness is a confused, unstable or bewildered mind. In some instances these traits can be symptoms caused by an underlying medical condition. But, for our purpose we will define confusion as difficulty focusing and maintaining attention in a way that interferes with the ability to make sound decisions and move forward in your life in a positive manner.

Confusion can be caused by many things including grief, depression, the loss of a job, spouse or loved one. These occurrences may leave one temporarily lost and adrift; wondering what to do next. This is a common and normal reaction to life's adversities. It is only when your circumstances cause you to feel that your world is being devastated and that your life has taken a suddenly, irreversible turn for the worse that confusion becomes a serious issue. A business associate and writer, Jacqueline Knight, relayed the following story to me:

Sharon couldn't believe the news she had just heard. Her hand was gripping the phone, frozen in time as the officer on the telephone told her that her son was dead; shot during a concert while away at college. It was a freak accident. A stray bullet had passed by thousands of other reveling young adults gathered in the parking lot after a rap concert, aiming narrowly at her son. Thomas had been sitting between two friends in the back seat of the car, when the bullet smashed into his brain, leaving his friends alive and unharmed. They didn't know who shot the fateful bullet.

For months on end, Sharon could do nothing more than cry at the memory of her oldest son. She reminisced about his youth and mourned the life he would never have. The idea of leaving her house was so repulsive to her that she completely cut herself off from the outside world. She ceased cooking for the family or interacting in any meaningful way; ignoring her husband, her other children, close friends and even the church. Nothing would ever be the same for her again. Her grief was so profound that she even contemplated taking her own life.

Almost a year later, I ran into Sharon. As we talked, I gingerly dodged asking her any questions about how she was feeling. I noted how lifeless she seemed. She was calm, but I wasn't feeling any peace from her. Not wanting to open old wounds, I took a chance and asked her if she would be willing to write an article on overcoming grief for a local, spiritual newsletter, and amazingly she agreed. For weeks, I worked with her on getting her thoughts, fears and hopes down on paper. When the article was released, dozens of men and women contacted Sharon to thank her for putting their feelings into words.

Several weeks ago, I ran into Sharon at a Thanksgiving event for the homeless. It had been at least three years since I had seen her. She was absolutely radiant and thanked me profusely for asking her to write the article. Not only did it help her to get her feelings out but also her real healing came as she helped others through their grief process. She told me that she had trained her mind to focus on the good things about her son and also on the good things that were still in her life. Today, she is counseling as a profession and has helped hundreds of others over the years.

The Untamed Mind

Short of the more drastic situation mentioned above, most confusion is a result of an untrained mind. A person with an untrained mind is like an amateur rider on the back of a wild horse that is bucking madly in an attempt to be free. For most of us, our lives exist at a frenzied, erratic speed that doesn't allow for calmness and peace. We wake up in alarm, run before work, rush to work, race through work, hurry home, make a quick dinner and "settle down" to the noise of the television. Quiet and tranquility are both unfamiliar and discomforting.

Our fast-paced world keeps our minds in chaos and understandably, some of us may constantly shift between anger, irritation, jealously and pride. We think these are the only mental tools we have available and this negativity contaminates our ability to think clearly and be at peace with ourselves.

We do not know or understand that the true source of success and happiness comes in the quieting of our mind, so we may start to blame the world for our dissatisfaction and failure. When we are in the habit of thinking like this, our mind has no choice but to harbor the fears and negativity that will inhibit our success.

When the focus is on how others around us are the cause of our unhappiness, "me..me..me" becomes our driving force. We get stuck on ourselves. We start to believe that superficial things outside of us will create happiness. One might begin to indulge in substance abuse believing that "this marijuana joint will make me happy or this drink will make me happy." Or, "this dress will make me happy or that car will make me happy." We may even turn our own bodies against us by thinking this chocolate or these potato chips will make me happy.

Self-obsession makes us small-minded and it repels the very energy we need to attract success. It is in this fertile soil that fear is born. Fear comes from the thought of not knowing *"what will happen to me?"* Inside of fear, the future is blurred. There is very little impetus to change a situation because we think what cannot be seen cannot be trusted.

At this stage, many of us can be fooled by the world of glitter, glamour and appearances. We may even live vicariously through the lives of the "stars" and come to consider the smallest and most irrelevant things important. We may become more interested in celebrity gossip than hearing or reading about how to bring about our own success and meaning to our own lives. We are living with minds gone wild!

 **Un-Doing the Confusion**

The process of undoing confusion is based on becoming aware and observant of what is happening inside your own head. Learning to stabilize confused feelings, emotions and impulses and to strengthen the mind with productive thoughts and ideas allows for a more insightful plane of truth, honesty and awareness.

Instead of living for our own needs, we need to grasp the reality that service to others ultimately brings happiness and success. There is not a single successful person that has not provided some type of service or contribution to the world. Bill Gates serves others by providing software that makes our lives and businesses easier to handle. Oprah Winfrey is successful because she provides information and entertainment for the enjoyment of others. Warren Buffet is successful because he helps others invest their money to improve their own lives and to live well.

Begin by changing your morning routine. Don't just jump up and begin blaring the radio or the television. Start your mornings by quieting your mind. The first ten minutes of each new day are very important. Use this time to set the tone for your day.

Training your mind is a crucial first step. A trained mind is like a tame horse. You tell it to go to the right and it does. You tell it to go forward and it does. Trying to achieve success without understanding this essential element is like wandering around aimlessly in a dark forest -- you'll need a light and a road map to get out. Either you control your mind or it controls you.

Irrational beliefs, Bad Observations, Faulty Perceptions

 Messages about life we send to ourselves that keep us from growing emotionally fall under the categories of irrational beliefs, bad observations and faulty perceptions or assumptions.

We have hundreds of hidden assumptions that we take for granted. These assumptions may or may not be true and very often we are locked into these biases, precepts and prejudices without knowing it.

They include scripts we have in our head about how we believe life **"should"** be for us and for others, as well as unfounded attitudes, opinions, and values we hold to that are out of synchrony with the way the world really is.

I have a cousin, quickly approaching the age of thirty, who dropped out of high school in the eleventh grade.

She claims she wants to be successful and happy but she cannot keep a job. Whenever she quits or is fired, it is always the fault of a manager or the supervisor.

Knowing she had a talent for hairdressing, her sister opened a hair salon and begged Helen to come and work with her. Helen would work sporadically coming in as she pleased. Ultimately, her sister had to take the opportunity away from her and give it to someone else.

Helen has a son and claims she wants to be in a good relationship. Unfortunately, she believes that there are "no nice men out there", so her couplings usually end in disaster.

In the last year, Helen has moved many times and finally moved back into mother's house. She constantly borrows money and accumulates frivolous charges on her Mom's credit card that she never repays.

Helen's biggest talent is knowing all the celebrity gossip. She can tell you who P. Diddy is dating and what kind of handbag Halle Berry carried to the Academy awards ceremony. It is of utmost importance to Helen to have all designer name apparel. She wouldn't be caught wearing an off brand. Where is Helen headed? What will happen to Helen if she doesn't change her perceptions and beliefs?

Helen is a good example of someone who carries a host of irrational beliefs, bad observations and faulty perceptions which include:

1. *Negative sets of habitual responses* that emerge when one is faced with stressful events or situations including stereotypic ways of problem solving in order to deal with life's pressures such as overeating, smoking cigarettes, abusing alcohol or drugs.

2. *Unproductive ideas, feelings, beliefs, ways of thinking, attitudes* opinions, biases, prejudices, or values from the past that we use when faced with problems in our current life.

3. *Self-defeating ways of acting* such as screaming, throwing things or manipulating a person or situation that only result in negative consequences.

4. *Counterproductive ways of thinking* that make you feel comfortable and secure but only aggravate the problem.

5. *Negative or pessimistic ways of looking at necessary life experiences* such as loss, conflict, risk taking, rejection, or accepting change.

6. *Emotional arguments for taking or not taking action in the face of a challenge* that usually results in no personal gain but rather in greater personal hardship or loss including being stubborn, bullheaded, intemperate, argumentative, or aloof.

7. *Ways of thinking about our selves that are out of context with the real facts* such as grandiose or self-defeating thoughts that result in our either under-valuing or over-valuing you.

8. *Confusion about the intentions of others* that develop when we are enmeshed in interpersonal problems with them.

9. *Lifelong messages sent to us either formally or informally by society*, culture, community, race, ethnic group, neighborhood, church, social networks, family, relatives, peer groups, school, work, or parents that are unproductive in solving our current problem or crisis, and we are either unwilling or unable to let go of them.

10. *Ritualistic ways by which we pursue our relationships with others* resulting in nonproductive relationships and increased emotional stress.

11. *Outmoded, unproductive, unrealistic expectations* exacted on us and/or others guaranteed to be unattainable. Thus resulting in continuing negative self-perceptions.

Irrational beliefs may be present if you get caught up in a vicious cycle when addressing problems. Some indications are:

1. Finding a continuing series of "catch 22's" that result in more or greater problems with every move you make to resolve your issue.

2. Suffering silently (or not so silently) with a problem for a long time; yet making no effort to get help.

3. Deciding on a solution to a problem yet finding you are incapable of implementing it.

4. Choosing a problem-solving course of action, being unhappy with the course, yet avoiding looking for alternatives.

5. Not pursuing a certain course of action because of the guilt or fear you will feel if you do it.

6. Being constantly obsessed with a problem yet taking no to resolve it.

7. Being immobilized and afraid to face your problems.

8. Avoiding, denying, ignoring, running away from or, turning your back on your problems.

9. Arguing both sides of your problem, and being unable to make a decision.

When you work under an irrational belief system, utilize bad observations or are cursed with faulty perceptions or assumptions, you fail to see the garden of potential options and possibilities that exist for you. You can become indoctrinated with the idea that you have no control over your life often to the point of believing that what goes on outside of you is more important that what goes on within.

CHAPTER TWO

Procrastination:
The Flat Tire That Leads to Failure

"People procrastinate because they are afraid of the success that they know will result if they move ahead now. Because success is heavy, and carries a responsibility with it, it is much easier to procrastinate and live on the "someday I'll" philosophy."

Dennis Waitley

CHAPTER TWO

Procrastination: The Flat Tire That Leads to Failure

*"No wonder you're late.
Why, this watch is exactly two days slow."*

Mad Hatter, Alice in Wonderland

So, What Are YOU Waiting For?

When people fail to reach their goals or live their dreams, one underlying reason is procrastination. Thousands of people will tell you they want to be rich. Nevertheless, they consistently put off doing the little things that need to be done in order to set themselves on the road to reaching their dreams. Doing the little things correctly, in a timely manner and in the right sequence is what makes success attainable.

With many of its roots based in our basic belief system and core values, procrastination is a multifaceted behavior that affects all of us to some degree. The dictionary defines procrastination as "intentionally and habitually putting off things that should be done." For some, it can be a minor problem. For others it is a source of significant tension and concern causing anxiety in many areas of their lives.

Procrastination is only somewhat related to time management, because procrastinators often know exactly what they should be doing at a given moment in time. Often, some procrastinators do not recognize that they suffer from this affliction. Burdening them with very detailed schedules and timetables is no help -- until something happens that gives them a rude awakening.

Bob, for example, knew that his company was downsizing and he didn't bother to look for another job until he was actually unemployed. Risking both his security and his family, he was not motivated to get on top of the situation

BEFORE the situation was on top of him. Or, Alice who procrastinated refinancing her home until the interest rates rose so high that the option to refinance became moot; costing her hundreds of thousands of dollars in interest payments. Both Bob and Alice passed up a prime opportunity to take control of their lives. Due to their procrastination, they ended up losing in a major way.

We all have a choice. We can just dream about reaching our goals or we can get up and take action! History records that Albert Einstein stayed up for days and days on end, tinkering with this and toying with that; trying it one way and then another before finding answers to his questions. Ultimately, Al was successful in his quests. Are you getting up early and going to bed late to find your solutions? Or are you sitting, dreaming of what could be?

Procrastination is a mental excuse for not trying. Some people don't try because they have a deep-seated, preconceived belief that they are going to fail. Henry Ford, the father of the modern automobile, once said, " Whether you think you can or you think you can't. You're right."

But…But…But…

"If and When were planted, and Nothing grew."
Proverb

Procrastinators come up with all sorts of excuses like, "I'll start when the weather breaks" or "I'll do it when the kids get older…" or "I don't have the right clothes…" or "It costs to much money…"

There was a time in my life when I suffered from a severe case of procrastination. I was a pro at it. I used all sorts of excuses as well as time-tested procrastinator tools to avoid my destiny. Thank God I got a " Hello! Wake Up!" call before it was too late.

I once had a supervisor by the name of Pat who was very good at the

extremely competitive sport of handball. One day, after cleaning my clock on the court, Pat asked me why I was still riding around in my old, ragged green car and not driving a Mercedes like him. My immediate response was that "a Mercedes cost too much money."

Pat stopped me in my tracks, looked me straight in the eye and said. "A Mercedes doesn't cost too much. You just can't afford one." It was then that a little voice inside of my head said, " Helloooo... Wake Uuuup... I had a choice. I could drive my green street beater, or I could find a way to afford that Mercedes. Excuses were in the way.

My procrastination was an avoidance behavior that allowed me to remain in my comfort zone. I felt safe not having what I considered to be a huge car payment even if it meant that I parked around the corner so no one could see what I was driving. It was uncomfortable to come in early and stay late at work. My procrastination allowed me to escape from what I considered to be unpleasant activities.

Today, I live joyously outside my comfort zone and encourage others to do the same. If you want something that you've never had, you have to be willing to do some things that you've never done. It's time to change your life!

Many people fail to see the garden of potential options and possibilities that exist and don't affect their reality in a consistent way because they are conditioned to believe that they have no control over our lives. They believe that what goes on outside is more important that what goes on within.

Four Motives for Procrastination

"Waiting is a trap. There will always be reasons to wait. The truth is, there are only two things in life, reasons and results, and reasons simply don't count."

Dr. Robert Anthony

1. ***It's too hard.*** It is natural to try and avoid tasks that seem impossible or question our abilities. When a child is learning to ride a bike, they may not be very accomplished in the  beginning. But, if every child gave into the fear of doing difficult things, a lot of us would never have learned to ride a bike. Falling down is a part of getting up.

2. ***It will take too much time.*** Time is a commodity we don't control. It is our job to use it wisely. If a task will take up a large block of time, we might put it off hoping that in the future, we will "find" the time. When we don't, it languishes in the "things I wish I had time to do" pile.

3. ***You don't know how.*** Making mistakes is inevitable and increases our knowledge curve. Don't be afraid to try something new. If you wait until you are an expert before you start, you may never begin. If you don't know something, take it upon yourself to learn it. Be courageous.

4. ***You're afraid to look stupid and everyone will know you messed up.*** Pride and ego can block us from trying things that might make us look silly or stupid. Often, fears are needless and when we put them aside and move ahead, we find that we can do the thing we are afraid of. Think about people who are afraid to go outside their homes. They are afraid of the things you face everyday; human contact, terrorist attacks, traffic jams, the sky falling down. When was the last time you got conked by a cloud?

25

Procrastination Thy Name Is ... Why?

"Procrastination is the grave in which opportunity is buried."
Author Unknown

 Two of the many traits that a procrastinator struggles with are low self-esteem and low self-confidence. He or she might insist upon a high level of performance, but they really feel that they are inadequate or incapable of actually achieving that level.

Recently, I began an undertaking to build a thirty million dollar, luxury, ten-story condo community in Mid-town Atlanta. Since it was my first venture of this magnitude, the bank told me, "Bruce we will lend you the money to build the condos but we would like you to joint venture with someone with more experience." I said, "No problem."

I hired Sam, an architect I was sure would do a great job. During the planning stages, Sam developed this preconceived notion that my partner was not going to approve of his work. So, at our initial team meeting, Sam says to my partner, "I know you are not going to want me to be the lead architect because companies like yours never do."

Well, I'll tell you that I was floored! This guy had the job and managed to talk himself out of a half million dollars. The next day I fired him. He was a procrastinator and his lack of confidence to do the job made me lack confidence in him. Other reasons that a procrastinator might use are:

- I'm Too Busy – Often used to call attention to how busy he thinks he is or how busy she wishes she was. There are so many important complicated affairs going on in life that he can't possibly do a decent job right now. Life is so demanding and there is so much going on that she couldn't attend that meeting. The procrastinator may waste time explaining why he or she cannot complete the task instead of spending the time performing the task at hand.

- <u>My Way or the Highway</u> – Sometimes used as an intellectual substitute for stubbornness or egocentric behavior. "I'll do it when I'm good and ready."

- <u>I Did it My Way</u> – Manipulation and control can be behind a procrastinator's action. "They can't do anything until I get there."

- <u>I Just Can't Take It Anymore</u> – Putting things off can feel good. But, it is not a good way to handle everyday pressures and anxieties. Someone else will eventually take on the activities and tasks that one fails to complete.

- <u>Woe is Me</u> – Some procrastinators live inside their victim mentality with no significant understanding of their own behavior. Since they won't compete or work like the "others." Someone must be "holding" them back

Seven Ways to Worry Less and Accomplish More

1. ***Know that procrastination bears its own unique fruit.*** The one sure thing that you can count on is that if you indulge in the fruits of procrastination, you will not be happy with the outcome.

2. ***Don't try to avoid activities you find unpleasant.*** You might be able to put off balancing your checkbook or paying your taxes for a time, but eventually you will come around full circle to face the task you thought you avoided only it will be laced with added penalties and interest.

3. *Avoid complacency and staying exactly where you are until the 12th of Never.* One sure way to accomplish nothing is to never try.

4. *Don't blame the world for your unhappiness.* You might be able to point the finger of your failure at your spouse, children, parents, boss or society in general. At the end of the day you will always know that you are the reason. Some people never accept responsibility for what happens to them. Ultimately your lack of success is your own burden, whether you choose to acknowledge it or not.

5. *Resist the urge to avoid failure by never trying.* Defeat is always temporary but giving up is permanent and difficult to resolve. Discover how to fail intelligently by learning from your mistakes.

6. *Get out of your comfort zone even if you are uncomfortable.*

7. *Don't try to win empathy from others or feel sorry for yourself.*

The Truth Behind Your Procrastination

"Procrastination is the bad habit of putting off until the day after tomorrow what should have been done the day before yesterday."

Napoleon Hill

When you begin to understand why you procrastinate, you will discover how to fix the problem. See if you can find a few of your procrastination traits inside Anna B's story.

Putting Off An Activating Event. Anna was an extremely talented writer; constantly in demand for her skills. When she put her mind to it, she could be wonderfully

imaginative and creative. Anna had always told herself that she could not write unless she came up with that first ingenious sentence.

In fact, she was convinced that unless that sentence came to her, she would not be able to write at all. At times, this served her well. She felt akin to a great writer, who once inspired could produce the "Great American Novel." But, at other times this worked against her because if she did not come up with that great first sentence she was lost and would never begin.

When Anna received a request from a national magazine to produce a compelling article on the foster care system, she was ecstatic – at first. This was her big break and could put her on the map among the other major magazines. It could lead to that book deal she so often dreamed about. But, then her procrastination demon kicked in.

Living with Faulty Belief Systems. For days Anna thought about how she would write the article and what she would say. She imagined her readers shedding tears of compassion from the very power of her words. But, every time she sat down at the computer to begin her article, she would stare at the computer screen waiting for that one great sentence that would send her off into a whirlwind of creativity. After a few minutes, her mind would wander to other "important" things. It was suddenly imperative that she completes the laundry or cleans the bathroom or any other chore that simply couldn't be put off any longer.

In the evenings, she couldn't take a break because she had to fix dinner or help the kids with their homework or watch a "can't miss" episode of "Desperate Louse Lives." At the end of the day, she was simply too exhausted to write. She would put off starting the article until the next day.

Deep down inside Anna was afraid to fail. As an overweight child, she had learned to hate ridicule, and she had a difficult time working with other students because she feared being ridiculed. When she felt nervous or pressured, she would simply put things off often giving up and never trying. Her belief system contained a host of negative feelings that controlled her responses to deadlines and pressure.

Career Killing Consequences. One month and three deadline extensions later, Anna had not written so much as one word. She never even started the article. Finally, her last deadline came and went, and still Anna could not come up with that first sentence. Eventually, the magazine cancelled her piece and Anna chalked it up to it "not being her time" for the big break. She even blamed the editor for not understanding that her creativity just wouldn't work under such stringent time restraints.

The consequences of Anna's actions had created an irrational approach to taking on difficult tasks. Rather than admitting to herself that she was scared, and moving beyond the fear, Anna gave into it and never gave herself a chance. If she had examined her belief system, she might have gained an understanding of why she delayed beginning certain things and possibly been able to change her way of thinking.

Are you clinging to faulty beliefs that are keeping you from achieving success?

But Wait!!! Why Should I Stop Procrastinating???

"Much of the stress that people feel doesn't come from having too much to do. It comes from not finishing what they started."
-- David Allen

 Procrastination makes you feel vulnerable, ineffective, and powerless. It drains you of motivation and keeps you trapped in a cycle of fears and excuses why you cannot achieve your best.

Procrastination feeds upon itself and reinforces your negative attitudes toward a task. It can destroy your personal life, hold you back in your business and career, and slowly eat away at your self-esteem as you watch others achieve while you maintain a status quo; or worse, go backwards.

When Bob received his pink slip that Friday, it was not exactly unexpected. He had known for nearly five months that BBF and D was going to be downsizing due to unexpected and catastrophic loses in the marketplace. He also knew that most likely the Marketing Department, his department, would be hit the hardest. He refused to think about it. He had hoped against hope that if he could improve his personal productivity; they might just decide to keep him on. Despite pleas from his wife to at least visit a personnel agency, Bob continued to bury his head in the sand until the fateful day had come.

He was amazed at the depth of emotion that he was feeling as he packed his desk. Hot tears fought to spill out, but he maintained his composure as he walked across the parking lot to his car. Once inside, he let his emotions out. It wasn't just losing a job that he had had at for nearly 15 years that upset him the most. It was not having a job to go to. "What was he going to do now? He hadn't saved very much money and it was going to be rough going until he found another job. He was forty-five years old, and

 *finding a decent job, competing against those young hotshots was going to be hard. Why, oh why did he wait so long to start looking for a new job? What was he so afraid of? Why didn't he take control of the situation sooner?"*

As he was pulling out of the parking lot, he saw his buddy Bill who had also been let go that morning. Bill had been one rung below him at the company, but they had become good pals just the same. He watched with curiosity as Bill loaded boxes into the back of his SUV. What he noticed was that Bill was smiling! He threw the car into park and approached his friend, determined to learn the reason for his high spirits.

What he learned was that in one week Bill would be taking over the Marketing Department at a competing firm. He had begun his job search the minute word came that layoffs were imminent. He had turned down lesser offers until he found a position that was better than the one he was losing and had walked away with a large increase in both position and salary.

By taking charge of his life and moving forward, Bill felt stronger, more competent, powerful and capable. By taking charge of your life, you will experience increased independence, personal freedom and peace of mind. You will be able to feast at the table of life instead of watching from the sidelines and picking up the crumbs!

Is There A Simple Cure?

NO! Procrastination is a self-sustaining habit. Every time you don't do something that you find difficult, you practice avoidance instead of participation. Procrastination strengthens your fears and keeps you from gaining new insight, training and skills.

Most procrastinators have been honing this habit their whole lives. The simple answer is to think that you can simply do everything opposite of what you are doing today; to tell you that the task isn't so hard or it won't take as long as you think. You can even tell yourself that you already know how to do it, or that you can learn while you're doing it. The fact is that, although it is possible to break old habits, it takes work.

If you don't have "The Success Within" workbook, take a blank sheet of paper and divide it into two columns. Think of things you are currently procrastinating about doing and write it at the top of the page. It might be personal, business or work-related.

Label column one "Reasons for Delay" and write down all the reasons that you use to procrastinate doing this task. Give this deep thought because some of your reasons might be hidden in your subconscious. Write down as many reasons that you can think of, using additional pages if you have a lot of excuses.

Label column two, "Arguments Against Delay." Write down every argument you can against the reasons for the delay. For instance, Alice was procrastinating on refinancing her house. One reason for delay was that she feared her credit wasn't good enough. Her argument against her delay could be until she pulled her credit, she really wouldn't know whether it was good or bad. With the knowledge of her credit score, she would be able to take the necessary steps to refinance.

Reasons for Delay	Arguments Against Delay

CHAPTER THREE

Between Fear and Faith

*"God has not given us a spirit of fear and timidity,
but of power, love and self-discipline."*

2 Timothy 1:7 NLT

CHAPTER THREE

Between Fear and Faith

"Don't let weeds grow around your dreams."

Howard Dobbs

Come On In. The Water's Fine.

The relationship between fear, faith and success is a concept that requires an intricate understanding of how things work in the metaphysical dimension and manifest in the physical world. Anyone who has ever been successful has had to have faith; whether that faith was on a conscious or subconscious level.

The common thread that runs through anxiety, worry, nervousness, irritability and depression are the colors of fear. While fear itself is a natural reaction to people, places or things that represent a threat; in its proper place, it is an essential tool for survival. Outside of its native element, fear can be a dangerous stumbling block that causing us to hesitate at critical moments.

Fear can be defined in a number of ways. Zig Ziglar defines it as "**F**alse **E**xpectations **A**ppearing **R**eal. According to Jacqueline Knight, entrepreneur, motivational speaker, writer, and public relations consultant based in Tampa, Florida, "The funny thing is that, what we are afraid of is usually something we think will happen to us at some undetermined time in the future." She goes on to say, "We are anticipating something negative that will most likely never happen. It's like the fear of failing a test before the teacher even puts it on the desk even though you know the material.

The fear of success is one of the most confusing of all possible blockades to accomplishing your goals and reaching your dreams. It usually arises when we are in the process of making changes and moving forward in our lives.

As a kid, I was really afraid of water. I can remember during swimming lessons, stroking along smoothly and treading -- until I looked around at my circumstances. I was in sixteen feet of water! Suddenly I would panic and begin to sink! I can't count the times I ended up sabotaging my efforts and nearly drowning myself, without realizing that I was actually swimming. Today, although I am still no fish, I have gotten this particular fear under control.

Fear is also a powerful driving force that can take over if it gets out of control. There was a time in my life when I was motivated and stressed out by the fear of having no money and being unable to pay my bills. When my negative motivation of fear changed to the positive motivation of wanting to be a philanthropist, the focus became more intense and the stress disappeared. With my mind redirected, I began to have faith in my ability to accomplish my goals.

When you have faith you can recognize your fear and keep going. Motivational speaker, Les Brown says "feel the fear and do it anyway."

It's a Matter of Faith

Faith is taking action based on your beliefs. It works regardless of the religion to which you subscribe. I have read many holy texts and studied what scholars and prophets have said on the issue of what we can do if we have faith.

One of my favorite definitions is, "Faith is the Substance of things hoped for, the Evidence of things not seen." I like this definition because it is, in essence, a scientific formula that will work for anyone regardless of their religion.

 *Like everyone else, Jab had received the news that the town was about to be*

flooded and that he should evacuate. Jab refused, saying the "Lord is going to save me." The water started to rise. Rescue workers came by rowboat and begged Jab to get in. Jab refused saying the "Lord is going to save me." The water continued to rise and forced Jab on the roof.

A rescue helicopter came by and dropped a lifesaver. Crew members begged Jab to put the doughnut around his waist, and hold onto the rope so they could haul him to safety. Once again Jab refused saying, "Lord is going to save me."

Jab drowned and went to Heaven. While passing through the pearly gates, he asked God why he had not saved him. God replied to Jab ..."What do you mean? I sent you a row boat AND a helicopter."

Having faith and believing are different concepts. You can believe but not have faith. Faith demands that you to take action.

My father once told me about a very religious woman named Gertrude, who was rushed to the emergency room of the best hospital in the city after being bitten by a very poisonous snake. As she lay in the hospital bed, the best doctor in the hospital gave Gertrude the serum antidote and told her if she drank it, would be cured.

The doctor asked Gertrude "Do you believe what I am saying to you?" Gertrude nodded that she believed and then proceeded to talk on and on for hours about her faith and how much she prayed everyday. Gertrude never did take the serum, and she died. She talked about her belief and faith but she never took action.

Whatever you want or need is already there for you. It is a Substance. It is Real. To manifest it ... to make it tangible is to take Action. You have to Act on it.

I think Ralph W. Emerson summed it up when he wrote:

What e'er in nature is thine own

Floating in air or pent in stone
Shall rive the hills and swim the sea
And like thy Shadow follow thee

The Landscape of the Mind

"If I had a world of my own, everything would be nonsense. Nothing would be what it is, because everything would be what it isn't. And contrary wise, what is, it wouldn't be. And what it wouldn't be, it would. You see?"

Alice: Alice in Wonderland

Our belief systems and the conclusions we come to are molded by our experiences as a result of what we have been taught throughout our lives. Whether we accept or reject a tenet or belief is dependent upon whether or not these new beliefs are in tune with our own life experiences.

Sometimes, because of experiences, we form irrational beliefs about ourselves, and the world. If you are functioning under an irrational belief system, you might feel that your success is undeserved and that the good things in life cannot possibly be yours.

If you have been abused in your lifetime -- mentally, emotionally or physically -- your beliefs about yourself and your relationship to the world might be based on those experiences.

Some people even believe that if they "get it together," no one will pay attention to them. If you have conditioned yourself to seek sympathy or you engage in chronic negativity, it will be nearly impossible for you to visualize yourself in a content, successful life.

Coming Out of the Shell

The fear of success is almost opposite of fear of failure because fearing failure is the fear of making mistakes and losing approval. Fear of success is the fear of accomplishment and being recognized and honored.

Are you afraid that no matter how successful you are, it will never be enough? Do you think that there are others who can replace or displace you at any time? If you answered yes, then you are living in a state of fear.

Do you fear that your achievements can be reduced to nothing at anytime? Do you lack a basic belief in your ability to achieve and nourish your progress? If you answered yes, then you are afraid of success.

Success is a continuing journey -- not the end of the road. When you move without fear, you are able to sustain interest and commitment to keep the trip exciting. Even when you have diligently worked for and achieved your goals, your motivation to continue to move forward will not fade.

The Fear of Success in Action

Many people who are afraid of success lack the motivation to achieve the goals they have set for themselves; in school, on the job, at home, in relationships, or in personal growth.

Fear of success can cause you to behave self-destructively, sabotaging your own achievements; being unable to solve problems or make firm decisions about your life; losing the motivation or the desire to grow, achieve, and succeed causing you to live in a state of chronic underachievement.

Often when one fears success there are also feelings of guilt, confusion and anxiety. Some people feel unworthy of success. This feeling of unworthiness causes them to falter, waver, and eventually lose momentum, sabotaging any gains they have made in their personal growth and mental health.

Overcoming Your Fear of Success

Learning to reinforce yourself for the hard work, effort, and sacrifices you've made to achieve success and being able to honestly appraise your level of achievement, success, and accomplishment is the first step to beating this particular fear.

You might be tempted, but don't make any excuses for being successful or unsuccessful. Accept yourself as being healthy, "together," happy, successful, prosperous, and accomplished

Give trusted others in your life permission to give you open and candid feedback when they see you self-destructing or backsliding. Monitor your level of commitment and motivation to reach your goals.

Visualize a successful life. See yourself as who you want to be. Make sure that you live a life that gives others credit, recognition, and support for their personal achievements, successes, and accomplishments. Most people don't affect their reality in a consistent way because they don't believe they can. Believe you can!

With balance poise and humility, be honest, open and realistic. Accept the compliments and recognition of others with an open heart and mind.

Dealing with Bad Habits

The dictionary defines a habit as *"a behavior pattern acquired by frequent repetition or physiologic exposure that shows itself in regularity or increased facility of performance."*

Bad habits are acts or methods followed with regularity and usually through choice. They are acquired modes of behavior that have become nearly or completely involuntary, repetitious, unconscious and often compulsive. In actuality, we choose our habits good or bad. The key to eliminating our bad habits is to identify and define them so that we can put more positive habits in their place.

Everyone has a tendency to repeat acts or processes. That is why some people will give preference to that which they have done before, or thought before, rather than to new ways of doing or thinking. A habit is marked by the propensity to deal with what is familiar.

There is a difference between an inconvenience and a problem!

Steps to Overcoming Fear of Success

You first need to identify the fear of success in your life. To do this, answer questions 1-10 for each of the following twelve areas:

1. At school	2. In your career
3. On the job	4. In your emotional life
5. With family	6. In your hobbies
7. In marriage	8. In sports
9. In relationships	10. In your physical health
11. With friends	12. In your spiritual life

1. What do I think will happen if I achieve success?
2. What would success in this area of my life look like?
3. In what ways do I feel undeserving of success?
4. Who am I afraid of hurting or intimidating if I achieve success?
5. What do I think will keep me from sustaining success?
6. What are my biggest concerns about succeeding in this area?
7. Who do I believe is more deserving of the success I will achieve?
8. How motivated am I in the struggle for success in this area?
9. In what ways do I think that once I achieve success, I will lose focus or direction in other areas of my life?
10. In what ways do I think that I'll be unsatisfied or feel unworthy if I achieve success in this area?

Overcoming Bad Habits

Step 1: a comprehensive list of what you consider to be bad habits that keep you from being successful. Think about what others have told you as well as what you believe. **Remember:** If you can't be honest with yourself, you cannot effect change.

1.	6.
2.	7.
3.	8.
4.	9.
5.	10.

Step 2: For each habit listed, decide what risks you are willing to take to release yourself from old habits. *(Example: I am willing to risk feeling uncomfortable for a short time to create a better future for my family)*

1.

2.

3.

4.

5.

6.

7.

8.

9.

10.

Step 3: List the Fears that you have about not being successful at breaking your old habits.

(Example: I will feel like a failure again)

1.
2.
3.
4.
5.
6.
7.
8.
9.
10.

Step 4: For each bad habit you have, list the corresponding **"good habit"** you would need to develop to offset it. For instance, if you regularly smoke, you might offset that habit by taking up regular exercise.

Bad Habit I Have	Good Habit I Need
1.	1.
2.	2.
3.	3.
4.	4.
5.	5.
6.	6.
7.	7.
8.	8.
9.	9.
10.	10.
11.	11.
12.	12.

Chapter Four

The Road to Success is Paved

"Rarely do we find men who willingly engage in hard, solid thinking. There is an almost universal quest for easy answers and half-baked solutions. Nothing pains some people more than having to think."

Martin Luther King, Jr.

Chapter Four

The Road to Success is Paved

On the Road Again

Before you pack for your trip to Successville, you will need the following essential tools: A definition of what constitutes success for you; an honest self-assessment; defined values, a clear vision, written goals and objectives, written strategies and a written personal mission statement. These tools will help you along your road to success.

You can realize success in one area of your life while missing the mark in another area. A self- assessment can give you more choices and broaden your options. Once you have discovered who you are and what you want, it will be easier for you to achieve a well-rounded life and have the confidence that you need to get on the road to success.

A self-assessment can reveal your characteristics, interests, values and skills. It will define your strengths and your weaknesses. You are the place to start. Ask yourself:

- What do I do well? What do I do that comes naturally? What do others tell me I do well?

- What do I enjoy doing? What turns me on? What energizes me?

Success requires hard work, passion, knowledge, self-awareness and courage. Some successful people enjoy talking about their success, especially to people genuinely interested in learning from their experience.

You can learn the ways of the business world by continually asking successful people question after question about how they got where they are, what mistakes they made along the way, and how they conduct their business.

What is Success?

"Winners do all the time, what others only do on occasion."

Bruce Dobbs

 Success is the accomplishment of a planned goal. It is a favorable outcome that may result in wealth, favor, happiness or eminence.

Success means different things to different people. It may mean a happy family life or the ability and lifestyle that allows for frequent travel or leisure time. It might mean managing the responsibilities that come with outrageous wealth and fortune. For many men and women, success is measured by what they give to the world and not what they take from it.

Many successful people have learned to identify important elements that help them on their road to success. They:

1. ***Have defined what success means for them***, and how they plan to achieve it.

2. ***Set achievable goals***.

3. ***Choose great teammates***.

4. ***Know how to make a decision***.

5. ***They self-talk***. Eliminate negative mind chatter and replace it with positive affirmations.

6. ***Have the courage to take action***.

7. ***Turn disappointments and failures into positive opportunities***. Many great successes are built on the graves of failures.

8. ***Keep going until the end***. Persevere! Do something each day that brings you closer to your goal!

9. ***They peg their strategy to a timeline***. They establish dates to accomplish key elements of their strategy.

Personality Plus!

One of the most important factors in determining your happiness and success is learning to understand your personality, characteristics and attitudes.

Personality Checklist

Following is a brief sample of the Personality Checklist. A complete list can be found in the workbook.

Personality & Characteristics	Story #							Total #
Section R	1	2	3	4	5	6	7	
Athletic								
Conforming								
Down-to-earth								
Frank								
Persistent								
Practical								
Rugged								
Self-reliant								
Stable								
Section R Totals								

Defining Your Values Systems

"Before you can inspire with emotion, you must be swamped with it yourself. Before you can move their tears, your own must flow. To convince them, you must yourself believe."

Winston Churchill

Your values are the ideals that guide your personal conduct, interaction with others, and involvement in your career. Like morals, they help you to distinguish what is right from what is wrong and guide you in conducting your life in a meaningful way.

When you are planning your business and personal life, your values need to be considered because they will influence your choice of occupation, type of company or business startup, corporate culture, work-family balance, social and community involvement.

For instance, if you value good health, you will make time for daily exercise and proper nutrition. If you value career satisfaction, you will take time to examine your values and make choices that are consistent with them. Your basic core values can be grouped into four areas:

3. *Material values*: How you feel about money and things.

4. *Personal or Perceived values:* Are you responsible, honesty, reliability, and trustworthy.

5. *Human/Social or Cultural Values:* Are you religious? What part does heritage play in your life?

6. *Work Values:* How do you work and relate to your co-workers, bosses, and clients.

Values Sampler

Personal Values	Cultural Values	Social Values	Work Values
Caring	Celebration of Diversity	Altruism	Autonomy
Courage	Ethnic roots	Diversity	Competitive
Creativity	Faith	Eco-conscious	Conscientious
Friendly	Linguistic ties	Equality	Dedication
Honesty	National ties	Fairness	Fair/Ethical
Honor	Regional ties	Family closeness	Loyalty
Independent	Tradition	Lovingness	Professional
Integrity		Morality	Punctuality
Spirituality		Reliability	Remunerative worth
			Team player

Write the Vision – Make It Plain!

 One of the most important components to bringing out the Success Within you is to clearly define your personal vision. What do you want to create of yourself and the world around you?

Similar to a corporate or personal mission statement, your vision statement is a brief, concise, and inspirational statement of what you intend to become and to achieve at some point in the future.

Your vision is the broad, all-inclusive big picture of your intentions. As part of your overall development strategy for your life and your business, it is the image of the goals that you want to reach and your aspirations for the future. At this point, your vision statement will not include your strategy. In a nutshell, your personal vision is what you want to be, do, feel, think, buy, own, sell, associate with, and impact by some date in the future.

Your vision must be unique and appropriate for you. The following Personal Vision Statement is *only an example*:

I am exercising regularly, and have completed by Master's Degree in Business. I have married my current girlfriend and we own a large home in the Hamptons. We are active in our church and financially comfortable with several income streams.

This sample addresses the physical, educational, emotional, social and career areas of this person's life. It's a *snapshot* of how the person sees himself and is written in the *present tense*.

Once you have completed the Vision worksheet, you are ready to turn your Vision Statement into an Action plan.

Vision Worksheet

Things I Really Enjoy Doing	What Brings Me Joy	The 2 Best Moments of My Past Week	3 Things I'd Do If I Won the Lottery
Horseback riding	My children's happiness		

Issues or Causes I Care Deeply About	My Most Important Values	Things I Can Do at the Good-to-Excellent Level	What I'd Like to Stop Doing or Do as Little as Possible

 ## If You Don't Know Where You Want to Go, How Will You Know If You Get There?

The difference between where we are (current status) and where we want to be (vision and goals) is what we do (target objectives and action plans or tactics).

In order to get to where you want to be, you must have goals. Your goals are **where** you want to be. Your strategies outline the steps you need to take to get there.

Your objectives are your signposts within your strategies on the road to Success. They define the makeup of the path you will take and help identify the rough spots. Your tactics detail how you will reach your objectives.

Your objectives and goals must be simple, time specific, consistent, measurable and achievable. They should be focused on results. Tactics focus on specific activity. When properly written, your objectives and tactics can be measured against a timeline. You should be able to compare your actual results against your time line to determine if you are on the road to achieving your goals.

Your goal might be to get a medical degree. Your strategy is to enroll in Morehouse Medical School by the end of the summer and your tactic could be to take a preparation course for the MCAT every other day for the next six weeks.

The Final Destination

Your goals must be specific and based upon your personal values. Now is not the time to generalize. You must know precisely what you want to do and where you want to be by a certain point in time.

A goal is a specific statement of what you hope to achieve within a specific period. It is both definite and realistic. Long-range goals can be accomplished through strategic planning.

Finding Your Way to Your Success

An objective is that specific step or milestone, which enables you to accomplish a goal. Your objectives are instructions about what you want to be able to do. Setting objectives involves an ongoing process of learning, research and decision-making. Knowledge of your inner self, your personality and your vision are vital starting points in setting objectives.

Review your results frequently and weigh them against your expectations. Use this analysis as a guide to reinforce strengths and eliminate weaknesses as well as for the next round of setting objectives. Goals and objectives structure a plan of action.

Examples of measurable objectives include:

- I will incorporate my company by January 1st of the New Year. Tactic: On Tuesday, I will write the secretary of state for an application.

- I will attend four business seminars over the next 6 months. Tactic: I will attend the business league lecture series on Friday morning.

- I will identify six potential customers and present business proposals. Tactic: I will get a copy of the country club member list by Thursday of next week.

- I will create a database listing of 20 companies to send marketing materials to over the next 2 months. Tactic: I will get Business Week magazine and research companies mentioned in the articles by next Sunday.

It is easy to measure these objectives. When you make your expectations clear, you know whether you have accomplished your goals.

CHAPTER FIVE

Mission: It's Possible

"The reason most people never reach their goals is that they don't define them, learn about them, or even seriously consider them as believable or achievable. Winners can tell you where they are going, what they plan to do along the way, and who will be sharing the adventure with them."

Denis Waitley

CHAPTER FIVE

Mission: It's Possible

Why Share the Vision?

Several years ago, a small advertising agency received the biggest contract in their history from a well-funded Internet IT startup. This contract could put their business on the map.

With only three months to prepare for a major presentation, the CEO put together a team of some of the brightest and most talented copywriters, graphic artists and creative minds in the industry. During their initial meeting, Mr. CEO divided the group into several teams including pre-production; responsible for pulling together the elements to implement the new advertising campaign; the Creative Team, whose job was to come up with brilliant ideas, logos and packaging for the client and post-production; their job was to follow up the advertising campaign and determine whether it was successful.

He had begun to delegate responsibility when one of the ambitious young executives asked the question, "Where exactly are we going with this idea?" Sure of his own course and plan for the account, the CEO replied, "Just do the job I give you, I'll take care of the rest of it."

Several weeks into the campaign, Mr. CEO suffered a heart attack and was hospitalized in an unconscious state. Once he was out of the picture, the teams began to argue about the direction Mr. CEO wanted the advertising and promotion campaign to take. The writers maintained that copy was important therefore they should take the lead and the other teams should follow their plan. The more artistic minds contended that it was the visual aspect of the commercials that were important and that even without

 words the public would understand their intent. Some in pre- and post-production felt that the packaging and the logo would be most important to the client.

Because Mr. CEO never shared his overall vision and mission with his staff, they were unable to agree on a united direction for the campaign. Without a common vision, the teams split up into several different factions; each determined to come up with their own unique presentation for the client.

On the day of the big presentation there was both a sense of nervousness and excitement. Each team felt that they had come up with exactly what the client would love. As the meeting progressed, the CEO of the startup was looking confused. Although each team had presented brilliant ideas, they were not cohesive with each other, often times even contradicting other team members. Before the meeting ended the folks from the IT startup had silently left the room. Needless to say, the advertising company lost what could have been a cornerstone client and went quietly out of business.

Two critical mistakes had been made: (1) not picking a second in command who shared his vision and (2) not sharing the mission and expectations with his entire staff.

Whether it's your family, your business or any other organization where you have leadership responsibilities, it is essential that there is an established and clearly shared vision and purpose, so that everyone knows exactly where they fit in and where they are going.

What is a Mission Statement?

"Man's reach must extend his grasp or
what's a heaven for?"

Albert Einstein

A Mission statement is a clear and succinct statement of purpose. It can be socially relevant highlighting ethical or moral positions, establish a public image, target a specific market or explain purposes for services or products.

Although you can create a mission statement for individual projects, ideas or ventures, there are two primary types of mission statements you need to create for yourself as you map out the road to your success. One is a single corporate or business mission statement and the other is a personal mission statement that addresses what you personally want to achieve in your life.

Creating A Personal Mission Statement

A personal mission statement addresses three questions:

1) What is my life about?

2) What do I stand for?

3) What action am I taking to live the life I stand for?

Your mission statement should include: what you'd like to accomplish or contribute, and who you want to be, and character strengths and qualities you want to develop.

Who is Living the Life You Most Admire?

Do you know anyone who is living or has lived a life that you admire? It doesn't need to be a friend, family member, business associate, or even anyone you know. Just a person or persons whose life most closely emulates the life you'd like to have.

Take some serious time and study this person, their background and history as well as their thoughts, ideals and lifestyle. If they've written any books, purchase them or borrow them from the local library.

Why Have a Mission Statement?

Mission Statements tell everyone, not only your clients, but, your employees, family, friends and anyone else you might care to share it with, what to expect, the character of your busines, and how your future decisions are formed. It is also critical because a Mission Statement can help you determine your position in relationship to your competitors as well as keep your vision on track.

Your Mission Statement is the guidepost that helps set your direction.

Developing a Mission Statement

Many successful businesses create their mission statement as part of their initial business plan. Some Mission Statements are short and to the point, while others are lengthy and detailed. Remember that everything you do should relate back to your basic mission and be in line with your goals and objectives.

If your business goals and objectives are fluid and changing, your mission statement may need to be rewritten many times over the years to take this into account. At the beginning of each year, you need to review your mission statement to make any necessary changes. Resetting your objectives and goals at the beginning of the year, will help keep your business fresh, new and on track for success. This is also true for your personal mission statement.

If you have employees, you can make developing your mission statement a team effort at a weekend retreats in a relaxed environment. A retreat can stir your creative juices and give you the necessary motivation to create an outstanding business mission statement. You can begin with words that describe the goal of your company and take off from there. Yearly weekend retreats to revise your mission statement can re-energize your team.

Conveying the Message of the Mission

Once you develop a mission statement, it is time to get the message out to your clients and your employees. You can print it on the back of your business cards, use it on your letter head, and definitely put it on your corporate website. You might also want to display your mission statement inside of a frame and place it throughout your office space.

Sample Mission Statements from the Corporate Big Boys

Here are some one liners used by some of the largest companies in the world:

3M -- "To solve unsolved problems innovatively"

Mary Kay Cosmetics -- "To give unlimited opportunity to women."

Merck -- "To preserve and improve human life."

Wal-Mart -- "To give ordinary folk the chance to buy the same thing as rich people."

Walt Disney -- "To make people happy."

Dream Big!

Your Mission Statement can be relatively simple using only immediately achievable goals, or it can be based on the wildest dreams for your company and your life. If you want to succeed big, you might want to start dreaming big!

Visualize the best you or your company can be if you achieved your mission and base your Mission Statement on that. Some business consultants will tell you that a Mission Statement should have a grand scale, be socially meaningful or relevant and be measurable. So, go ahead, live your Mission Statement on the grandest scale you can envision, but make sure that you can measure your progress.

Following are a few examples of Mission Statements that were large and seemingly impossible to reach:

Ford Motor Company (early 1900's) --"Ford will democratize the automobile"

Sony (early 1950's) -- "Become the company most known for changing the worldwide poor-quality image of Japanese products"

Boeing (1950) -- "Become the dominant player in commercial aircraft and bring the world into the jet age"

Wal-Mart (1990) -- "Become a $125 billion company by the year 2000"

CHAPTER SIX

Building Your Success Team

"Life is too short to spend your precious time trying to convince a person who wants to live in gloom and doom otherwise. Give lifting that person your best shot, but don't hang around long enough for his or her bad attitude to pull you down. Instead, surround yourself with optimistic people."

Unknown

CHAPTER SIX

Building Your Success Team

Cheerleaders and Coaches

One of the most important things you will do on your road to success is surround yourself with an effective support and networking team. This doesn't mean that you need to go out and hire a full time staff but you should have people around you who recognize your abilities and support your dreams financially, emotionally and idealistically.

Whether your support team members are family, friends, business acquaintances, mentors, business consultants or coaches is up to you. It is good, however, to have a balanced mixture of people including those who know you well, and those who can see your vision more objectively. Your team members must believe in and be committed to your success.

Family Ties

Members of our family can be your biggest supporters, or your biggest detractors. Carefully evaluate each family member's attributes before you assign them a responsible position on your Success Team.

Families can work together if they treat the family business as a business and do not take advantage of the fact that their boss may be a younger sibling, cousin or aunt. Don't be afraid to treat working family members as you would any other employee even to the point of letting them go if they become a detriment to your vision.

Cheryl Scales founded MySassySassy after being downsized from a major corporation. Her idea was simple: to design and produce a line of designer shoe insoles that she referred to as "shoe lingerie."

A true shoe diva, Cheryl designed a product from a need she had and correctly perceived that other women had this need as well. Pouring every spare dime into production, she was able to soft launch her project in the fall of 2005. The public response was immediate and Cheryl began fulfilling orders in the first month of production. Her fulfillment staff: Mom, Dad, nieces and nephews; a real family venture!

Her mother designs the beautiful boxes and bows that Cheryl uses when shipping her product, and everyone else pitches in filling those boxes.

Note: When you start a business, make it something that you are interested in and passionate about. If you love what you are doing, you will attract the people, resources and outrageous opportunities that will make you successful.

In the Huddle

Before you begin building your support team, you must first identify the areas where teamwork is needed. If you are manufacturing a product but have never been involved in manufacturing before, you need to find someone with the skills to teach you about the business.

If you know that your product or service will be marketing driven, or will depend upon Internet sales, then you should surround yourself with people who can help you set strategy or have the technological skills to assist you in your quest.

When building an effective support network, you should consider the basic skills you will need. When choosing your team members they should have one or more of the following four basic traits:

1. *The Industrialist.* Ideally, this person is you with your passion, vision and creative problem-solving abilities.

2. *The Manager.* This person is able to strategize, analyze and organize.

3. *The Designer.* This person can take your individual goals and help you translate them into corporate or group goals.

4. *The Worker.* This person knows how to get things done.

Birds of a Feather

"Don't make friends with an angry man, and don't be a companion of a hot-tempered man, or you will learn his ways and entangle yourself in a snare."
Proverbs 22:24

While on your quest for success, remember to surround yourself with positive people. One of the most distracting things that you can do to hinder your success is to allow someone who is either too pessimistic or just doesn't believe in you into your inner circle.

Callie is a very nice person. She is sharing, caring and ambitious.

Unfortunately, Callie's friends from high school were lazy, negative, scandalous and criminal. Because Callie had known her two friends for so long, she often went along with them when they invited her for a night on the town because she felt a sense of loyalty. She felt that if she did not go along that her old friends would no longer like her.

One day, while with these friends at a trendy store inside an upscale mall, unbeknownst to Callie, one of her friends attempted to shoplift a very expensive sweater.

While walking out of the store, the friend who had stolen the sweater and put it in her bag asked Callie to hold her bag as they were exiting the store.

The security buzzer went off, and Callie along with her scandalous friends were placed under arrest. Callie now has a criminal record she did not earn and has a difficult time finding a job.

Callie recently relayed to me that on one of her job interviews, the interviewer told her that her integrity would always be in question.

Remember: The quality of your life is directly proportional to the quality of the people in your life. Choose wisely.

It is of utmost importance that you surround yourself with highly motivated and positive people. My mother used to tell me, "You are judged by the company you keep." This is not to say that you should hide from negativity but negative people should certainly not be those with whom you consult, mentor with, or ask advice of.

Avoid the Haters

Rachel was very excited about her new look. She had lost more than 100 pounds during a grueling diet and exercise plan that her doctor had demanded she partake in or suffer lasting health affects. She changed both her hairstyle and her wardrobe to fit the "new" Rachel.

The first time her friend Adrian made a sarcastic remark about her new look, Rachel glossed it over as a bit of jealousy. But, now two months later, the jabs had increased in both frequency and contempt.

Rachel and Adrian had been best friends since meeting in prep school. They had attended the same college and shared six apartments over the last decade. The two traits they had in common were their love of food and mutual hatred of exercise.

Because they were always together, they had managed to put a wall between the world and themselves, especially when it came to their weight. Together they had shared countless late nights over pizza, wings, ice cream and soda complaining about their flabby this or too fat that.

During a routine physical, Rachel's doctor had informed her that if she didn't lose weight, she would inflame a heart condition that in a smaller person would not be life threatening. He prescribed an eight-week stay at a health spa to help get her weight under control and psychological counseling to give her self-esteem a boost.

Her stay at Health Heaven was the longest stretch of time she had been away from friends and family in her entire life. At first she was frightened without the creature comforts she was accustomed to. She also missed her best friend. But after a few days she met Carole who became both her mentor and her friend. When the going got rough, or she felt she couldn't survive another day, it was Carole's positive outlook that helped her over the rough spots. They had kept the promise to meet weekly at the gym to give each other support on the path to healthiness.

During lunch one afternoon, Rachel revealed to Carole that she was becoming aggravated with the way that Adrian was treating her. It was to the point that Rachel had even considered gaining a few pounds if it would make her best friend happy with her again. She found the idea frightening, but she was coming to a crossroads where Adrian was concerned and she knew she had to make a tough decision.

The next day, Rachel found an apartment not far from where she worked and by that weekend had moved out of the one she shared with Adrian. A year later, Rachel is on target with her weight. She is extremely happy and

*planning her wedding to Jeff, another former fatty that she
met at the gym.*

*She still sees Adrian on occasion, but mostly when their
families get together. Today, her friends share her sunny
outlook on life. And although, she misses her former best
friend, her life is well rounded and happy.*

The analogy is to a bucket of live crabs: Whenever one
crab attempts to escape the bucket by climbing out of it, the
others reach up and pull it back down. The result, of course,
is that no crab succeeds in escaping the bucket. Avoid the
crabs around you. Find successful, motivated people and
spend your time with them. Don't let anyone steal your
dreams from you or keep you from reaching the top!

Mentor Me!

 One of the most valuable assets in your life
or career is a good mentor. Webster's
dictionary defines a mentor as "a trusted
counselor or guide. The term Mentor
actually comes from a character in
Homer's poem "The Odyssey."

When King Odysseus left Ithaca to fight in the Trojan War,
he delegated the day-to-day operations of his monarchy to
Mentor who was the teacher and administrator of
Odysseus's son, Telemachus.

A mentor is an individual, usually older, always more
experienced, who helps and guides another individual's
development. This guidance is not done for personal gain.

Mentoring is used in many settings. Although it is most
common in business, mentors are often used in educational
settings, especially with "at risk" students. It is also the
basic principle behind the Big Brothers and Big Sisters and
Girls and Boys Club programs.

Your mentors will be the most important members of your
Team. In fact, your mentor should be able to help you pull

together the rest of the team as you learn and grow under their tutelage.

Many Mentor/Protégé relationships are often developed over time with people one might know, trust or have confidence in. But, this is not always the case.

A good mentor will offer you encouragement, support and advice while helping you to learn from your mistakes. They are close enough to you to help you build upon your strengths but distant enough to help you identify your weaknesses.

If your mentor is in the business arena, he or she can introduce you to important contacts and help set up collaborative partnerships while guiding you to financial independence.

Finding Your Muse

"When the student is ready, the teacher will appear."

Unknown

There are many different areas where you might find the need for a mentor including personal, business, spiritual and even your health.

You may find your mentor at a community meeting, health club, association, church, temple, mosque, or cultural affair. Your mentor might even be a neighbor.

Is there someone you admire or aspire to emulate? Has anyone impressed you with his or her intellect and business savvy? Maybe it's someone you've worked with in the past?

Let's say you don't know anyone who can fill the mentor role in your life. How do you go about finding one?

There are several Internet websites that offer free mentors. Of course your mentor may or may not live in the same city. I have mentors in the United States and in other countries. as yourself, and it is not absolutely necessary. I have several mentors who live throughout the United States and the world.

The Small Business Administration (SBA) and The Service Core of Retired Executives (SCORE) both offer entrepreneurs free mentor services as well workshops and seminars. Score also offers email mentoring online and a database of their available mentors.

Before deciding on a mentor, do a little research. Using either your workbook or a blank piece of paper do the following:

1. Decide which areas of your personal or business life require the assistance of a competent mentor. Define your top goals for the mentoring relationship.

2. Develop a list of prospective mentors. Research available information about them. Select the top candidates who share your goals.

3. Write a letter and request a meeting. You don't have to say that you are interested in a longer-term relationship, just that you are interested in getting their input.

4. Prepare a short list of questions soliciting their feedback on your current situation.

5. Meet with them. If they're willing to take time away from their office. You pick up the tab.

6. Ask them about their history, situation, and goals. State your goals and ask your questions. *Take notes!*

7. If you like their responses test the waters regarding a mentoring relationship. Would you be willing to meet with me again next month to follow up on what we've discussed today?"

8. Send a thank-you note. Rarely done. Always appreciated.

9. If you are interested, call to discuss the results of those actions and request a second appointment

10. Suggest a mentoring relationship. Be sure to make your goals and expectations clear.

11. Use the chart from the workbook to record your information.

Being Coached to Success

 A business coach can fill the same role in your life except for one important difference. A mentor assists you without personal gain, a business coach is a paid consultant.

Most business coaches do not give you packaged answers about what you should do to become successful. Instead they "coach" you in finding the answers. Some will conference with you while others will assign exercises that can help clarify your thinking process.

Choosing a coach can be a daunting task. Before you hire a coach you might ask yourself the following questions:

Where am I going with this? What style of coaching do I need? Am I addressing a business need: Or am I looking for a life coach who will help me with a variety of business and personal matters? Do I want a taskmaster, a sounding board, or someone who helps me see things differently?

How do I feel with this person? What you learn from your coach will depend on how the two of you get along. Whether your coaches are male or female, they must be someone with whom you feel comfortable with and someone that you trust.

Does this stuff make sense? You wouldn't ask a beggar how to get rich, so, why would you choose a coach who is not successful in his own life. How can your coach assist you?

Is he or she qualified? Coaches come in all shapes and sizes and from a variety of backgrounds. Ask for references as well as qualifications. Check out professional coaching organizations, and industry practices and standards.

How much does it cost? The cost for a coach can be as little as nothing or it can get very expensive. If you plan on making a decision based on the cost, remember the old adage, "Caveat Emptor: Let the buyer beware!"

CHAPTER SEVEN

Overcoming Setbacks Is A Part of Life!

"Trials, temptations, disappointments -- all these are helps instead of hindrances, if one uses them

rightly. They not only test the fiber of character but also strengthen it. Every conquering temptation represents a new fund of moral energy. Every trial endured and weathered in the right spirit makes a soul nobler and stronger than it was before."

James Buckham

Chapter Seven

Overcoming Setbacks Is A Part of Life!

Nobody's Life Is Perfect

No matter who you are, what you have done in your life, what you have or where you may have come from, at some points in your life and career it is a given that you will experience disappointments, difficulties, delays, struggles and setbacks as an inevitable part of being a living, breathing human being.

Whether at the pinnacle of success or are at the beginning of the road to your dreams, it is likely that things will not necessarily go your way, or worse yet, things will go woefully awry. A setback could be as simple as failing to make a routine sale or as pivotal as losing a really important client or deal.

One might struggle through the loss of a loved one through death or divorce, or it might be that a favorite pet has runaway. But, no matter how big or small our setback might seem at the time, it is important that we face each situation with a positive attitude remembering that setbacks are not personal insults and should not be taken as such.

Just because you have had one disappointment, or even a dozen, it does not mean that you have failed as a human being. If we become fixated on the negative, living in blame, rehashing a negative event or constantly complaining, we only rub the suffering in.

Our inability to let go may take us on a downward spiral into depression and self-pity. If you reach a point where your loss is taking you into despair... STOP! Take a deep breath and realize what is happening. You may need professional help. I address the issue of serious depression in more detail in the next chapter, Abundant Living.

If you do not feel that you need professional help and the vicissitudes of life have knocked you down temporarily, then ask yourself the following questions: Are my complaints in this situation legitimate, or am I complaining just for the sake of complaining? Am I blaming others for something I brought upon myself? What can be learned from experiencing this setback? What is it that I can do to change the situation? How can I overcome this obstacle?

Another way to deal effectively with setbacks is to find humor in the situation. Do not let your mind become imprisoned by setbacks. Endeavor to see the brighter side in every situation. As mentioned earlier in the book, a good support team can get you through almost anything, so always be careful when choosing the people that you want around you. Beware of "fair weather" friends.

Do Not Become Inert Matter

Know that you will have sleepless nights. Pain and disappointment are a part of life. I guarantee, they will come. And when they do come, realize that it is your time. When you have been knocked down, like a champion prize fighter, it is wise to take a step back and take a count for a few seconds. Take a breather.

When you lose, learn a lesson. Make the best of a bad situation. Go to a movie. Go out to dinner. Visit a museum. By doing this, you will give yourself time to come back and approach things with a fresh perspective. It is my understanding that when the captain of a sailboat is in the midst of a raging storm, he pulls down the sails and rides out the storm.

When the storm subsides, he sets his course, puts the sails back up and continues on his way.

Sometimes You Just Have to Let Go!

 If you are burdened with too much and there are not enough hours in a day, then eliminating or delegating some of your tasks will help you get a handle on your current crisis.

You can't do everything alone, and if you look around you might find that there are other people who are willing to help. Take a fresh look at what you think you have to do. You may find that some things are not necessary or can be delayed until a later time. When you are in the middle of a setback, reducing stress is critical to your survival.

All of us have 24-hours in a day. A good day planner is essential. Plan your day the night before. Beware of time thieves; people or things that burn up your time with trivia or foolishness.

You've Got To Have Friends!

There is nothing like having someone you can talk with. Setbacks can be discouraging and you can't allow your frustrations to build to the point where you are making irrational decisions. Having a trusted friend who can give you valuable input, suggestions and advice is as important as having the support of your family. Sometimes, we are tempted to lay everything on a significant other or take our frustrations out on our closest family members. Don't do it!

There is Nothing Like Being Prepared!

Knowing that setbacks are possible is your first defense against an unexpected obstacle. When you start a business, take a new job, or start a new relationship be realistic! It is possible that some things may not go your way. If you know this ahead of time, you will be able to handle the rough patches.

Change Begins with You!

Handling or avoiding setbacks in the future may require that you change your habits and behaviors. If you are willing to dream big dreams, then you should also be prepared to make the necessary changes in your lifestyle and personal habits that will cultivate an atmosphere of success in your life. Make a decision about the kind of life you want to live. Every day do something that will bring you closer to your desires. If you make proactive behavior a habit, you will achieve your success – one step at a time.

Learn to Pace Yourself

If you know your limitations and your skill level and you pace yourself to what you are able to personally handle, you won't have to worry about over extending yourself. A key reason why some people experience difficulties and setbacks is their failure to build a solid foundation. You cannot build the second floor before you build the first. Remember the old axiom: How do you eat an elephant?

Answer: One bite at a time! Never bite off more than you can chew and you won't have to worry about choking!

In A Nutshell: Get a Handle on Stress

If you are living and breathing you will experience stress in your life. You need to know and understand that you will face adversity and that temporary setbacks are inevitable. You will not win every battle. You will not get every job or win every bid. You will have sleepless nights and you will make mistakes. When you make mistakes, learn from it and move on. Never dwell on your limitations but focus only on your possibilities.

When things are not turning out as you planned, you should take a mental break from it all. Go for a walk, take in a movie or enjoy a dinner out. Try to clear your mind and give yourself a break. This will allow you to start fresh with new ideas.

Remember that not every obstacle is a bad thing. Sometimes not getting what you want can be a blessing in disguise. Several years ago, I put together a deal to buy the Atlanta Hawks, the Atlanta Thrashers and the Turner South Network.

I had a signed deal memo in hand, but due to circumstances beyond my control the deal went to another party. I was extremely disappointed at the time. I couldn't believe that I had missed the mark. I didn't achieve my goal. I felt like I had lost.

But now I am so glad that that particular deal did not manifest itself. Today, those teams are beset with mountains of problems that were not readily apparent when I was trying to acquire them. Not only did I avoid a major headache, I am not saddled with the financial burden that the current owners have. Sometimes not getting what you want, can be a blessing in disguise.

Chapter Eight

Living the Abundant Life

It had long since come to my attention that people of accomplishment rarely sat back and let things happen to them. They went out and happened to things."

Elinor Smith

Chapter Eight

Living the Abundant Life

To Your Health

"Good health and peace of mind are more valuable than anything else you can have in this world."

Howard Dobbs

One of the most overlooked topics when discussing achievement is the correlation between good health and success. I'm not saying that only healthy people are successful or that you won't be a success if you don't take care of yourself, but, what is the point of achieving your dreams if you unable to enjoy them because you have ruined your health.

Good health and wellness are about more than simply being free of illnesses or diseases. It is comprised of a variety of things including soundness of body and mind and our relationship to our family, friends, careers and jobs.

Stress: The Success Killer

In this fast-paced world, I think that stress in its various forms is the number one killer of success. Stress is a bodily reaction to a mental, physical, emotional or social stimulus that we respond to in a way that changes the way we feel, think or perform our daily tasks. Although stress is often treated from a psychological perspective it can also have physical side effects.

When we are stressed we cannot think straight, function efficiently or make good decisions. It would be nice if we could avoid stress and anxiety; nevertheless, it is unrealistic to believe that we can.

Under stress some people will drink or smoke to excess (although any smoking is excessive) or engage in other destructive and negative behaviors. Some people are prone to creating stressful situations in their lives while others simply stress over any and everything. For some people, stress itself is the addiction.

The results of stress can be mild or much more serious including high blood pressure, fatigue, irritability, chronic headaches, memory loss, tooth-grinding, insomnia, changes in appetite, skin disorders, infections, neck and back pain, low self-esteem, withdrawal, cold hands, shallow breathing, lowered sex drive, nervous twitches, changes in sleep patterns and gastrointestinal disorders.

Stress can interfere with your immune system and is said to be a contributing factor in all illnesses including cancer, heart disease, diabetes and other endocrine/metabolic diseases. In addition, stress can also be a source of psychological problems, anxiety and depression.

The following suggestions should be used to gain and maintain good health:

Nutrition

Everyday we ingest a variety of foods that can be harmful to our health and well-being. They include foods that are salty, fatty, and sugary as well as those that contain a host of artificial flavors and coloring. It would be wonderful if we could get the vitamins and nutrition from our food, but often what we eat is not providing us with what we need. It sometimes becomes necessary for us to supplement our foods with a good multi-vitamin/mineral everyday.

You should eat foods that are high in fiber including fruits, vegetables and whole grains. Avoid "smash and grab" eating and have at least one or two nutritional meals a day.

Avoid or lessen your intake of processed foods including artificial sweeteners, carbonated soft drinks, junk foods, sugar, white flour products and foods containing preservatives.

Exercise and Physical Activity

 Regular exercise will help keep your mind clear and stress under control. It will make you feel better about yourself and provide you with the strength you need while on the road to your success. Whether you join a gym, walk, jog or run; working out should become a part of your regular routine.

I spend three hours a week studying and training Tiger Crane style Kung Fu. I also assist my Surfu, Gary Mitchell, teaching a Kung Fu class every Saturday morning. On the days that I am not training, I spend a minimum of an hour lifting weights, stretching or running.

The mental and physical stress I consciously put my body through while practicing Kung Fu, makes it easier to deal with the slings and arrows of everyday life.

This is what works for me. Find what works for you.

Overweight

If you feel you are overweight; if your friends and family are expressing concern about your health because of your weight, or if your doctor has told you that you need to lose weight, then you definitely want to consider going on a diet and pay attention to your eating habits. I don't advocate any diet plan over another, but I will tell you that obesity can cause a myriad of health and emotional problems that can get in the way of your success.

Rest and Relaxation

It is important that your body get the optimal amount of rest that it needs to function. Health experts suggest anywhere from 6-8 hours a night for most adults and possibly more for teens and children. There are a variety of relaxation techniques that you can use to lessen body tension.

If you continually wake from a night's sleep feeling tired. lethargic and tense you should consult a doctor to find the best remedy for your fatigue. Tiredness and fatigue can lead to a weakened immune system and a greater chance of becoming ill.

Regular meditation and deep breathing techniques have been known to help people relax and handle stress. Watch your caffeine intake. It can disrupt sleep and contribute to nervousness. You should also avoid tobacco and alcohol.

Sometimes simply taking a day off to do something relaxing that you enjoy or pursuing a hobby that allows you to spend time with yourself can give you the break you need to refresh your mind, body and spirit.

Mind Control

As I mentioned earlier in the book, monitoring your internal conversations and paying attention to the way you talk yourself is directly related to how you feel about yourself as well as our environments.

Learn to recognize what you are feeling. Analyze your emotions. Accept that you are human and govern yourself prudently.

Get quiet! Strive to make your home and personal spaces a sanctuary from the world. Turn off the television, radio or stereo. There are also certain colors that can calm and sooth you. Use as much natural light in your home as possible.

Just as meditation works, Prayer is another source of relief. If life becomes too much, you might try a visit to a church, temple, mosque, synagogue or spiritual center. Sometimes simply reading from religious texts such as The Holy Bible, The Torah, The Koran or others can help.

A Personal Aside

I thought long and hard about including the following thoughts because the subject is touchy. However, since these are my conveyances about what I know to be true about being successful in life, at the risk of ostracism, I will share my personal thoughts on religion.

I believe there is a belief system that takes into consideration all the religions of this world. In this realm, there is a common thread that runs through us all. Whether we call ourselves Christian, Jewish, Buddhist, Muslim or Hindu, the common thread is woven in the fact that we are all human beings. As human beings it is the present knowledge of our sameness that should be celebrated. Our humanity should trump all differences we may have because of a professed religion.

The concept of Faith is not endemic to one religion only. Faith is a human phenomenon and works no matter what denomination you call yourself.

I recently heard a motivational speaker who had very good points to share with his audience. He concluded with, "And if you don't believe in 'XYZ' religion these principles won't work." Not only was I insulted, I was embarrassed for the couple next to me. They were clearly not of his religion.

Religious fanaticism has been one of the chief causes of human suffering and slaughter. It is the close-minded fanatical belief that "my way is the best and only way" that destroys our ability to reason with one another. This group doesn't like that group and this set of the next group doesn't like the other subset of the same group. What nonsense!

I was raised under a particular religious umbrella because of the location of my birth on this planet. If I were raised on the other side of this planet, I would have been raised under a different religious umbrella.

It is said that if a man does not stand for something, he will fall for anything. I stand for human rights. I truly believe that all men ... all men ... are created equal and have the right to life liberty and the pursuit of happiness.

Depression is very real

I touched briefly on the topic of depression earlier, but I feel that this is an important topic and should be taken seriously.

Serious depression is a medical condition often caused by an imbalance of brain chemicals, along with other factors and it needs to be treated. There is no shame in seeking professional help.

The symptoms often appear dichotomous: Sleeping too little or sleeping too much; rapid weight loss or rapid weight gain; eating too much or eating too little; lack of concentration and difficulty making decisions; thoughts of death or suicide; increased restlessness and lack of energy or motivation.

I have a very, very dear friend who suffers from depression. In the beginning, I did not realize that it is not as easy as telling them to "just snap out of it" or "look on the bright side." The problem is, they cannot "just snap out of it" and there is no bright side for them.

Although, depression can be treated through medication and psychotherapy, if you have a friend that is depressed here are some things you can say, and mean, to show your support: "I love you. I care. I cannot fully understand what you are feeling, but I want you to know that I am here for you. If you need a friend to talk to, I'm here."

Laughter IS the best Medicine!

"A day without laughter is a day wasted."

Charlie Chaplin.

According to a study by Hodge Cronin and Associates, 98 percent of the 737 corporate CEOs interviewed said they prefer to hire someone with a sense of humor to someone without. People tend to gravitate towards individuals who can find humor in tense situations and in life. According to several surveys, a sense of humor is one of the top traits that people seek in another person and is good for business and promotes good health.

Humor can give you a sense of power in a situation where you might feel you have no control. Laughter keeps your morale high and is a welcome addition when working with a group or a team. Not only is laughter a great stress reducer, it can diffuse tensions when things aren't going quite the way you planned.

According to a Ceridian Connection online article, *"Business success: A laughing matter"*, fifteen minutes of unrestrained laughter can have the same relaxing effect on the body as six to eight hours of meditation stimulating the respiratory and cardiovascular systems, relaxes muscles, reducing blood pressure and strengthening the immune system as well as combating depression and anxiety.

Dear Reader:

The advice in this book will assist you as you travel the road to success. This book is a key to open the door to the *The Success Within* you!

One thing I know is that to *Be In It To Win It!* you have to be fully committed. In a breakfast of ham and eggs, the chicken is involved... the pig...is fully committed! I am committed and I pray that what I have laid out in the pages of this book will lead you to *The Success Within*.

To reach out and grab your dreams, you need to have a positive attitude, coupled with an intense desire and a willingness to give it your all,. After hearing a Virtuoso perform an absolutely incredible piece, a woman said to her, "I'd give my life to play like that." The "Virtuoso" replied, "**I did!**" I urge you to build a success library and to attend seminars and workshops that will help you in your quest.

I have had great victories and great defeats and when I feel like I need a lift, I remember that Winston Churchill said, "Success is the ability to go from one failure to another with no loss of enthusiasm. Benjamin Disraeli said, "The secret of success in constancy of purpose." An old Chinese proverb states "a diamond cannot be polished without friction nor the man perfected without trials."

I am available for consultation and conversation – and I mean that. I know that sometimes in order to have outrageous results – it takes uncommon commitment.

I look forward to helping you learn and grow. Here's to you and your success!

Bruce Dobbs
President
Be In It To Win It, Inc.

Partial Bibliography

1. "Business Success: A Laughing Matter." The Ceridian Connection online article.

2. "Mission Statement", Business Resource Software, Inc., The Center for Business Planning

3. "Using a Personal Mission Statement to Chart Your Career Course" by Katherine Hansen, QuintCareers.com, 2006

4. "Education Leadership Toolkit" National School Boards Foundation, Institute for the Transfer of Technology to Education

5. "Is a Fear of Failure Stopping Your Success?" Elizabeth Johnson, Ezinearticles.com, 2006

6. "Choosing a Mentor," Larry Ambrose. Article, American College of Healthcare Executives.

7. "Discovering Your Talents," Brian Tracy. Article.

8. "Ten3 business ECoach" by Vladimir Koltelnikov. Website.

9. "Steps to Overcoming the Fear of Success," Tools for Personal Growth: Coping with Life's Stressors," Coping.org

10. Seneca Career Resources: ilearn.senecac.on.ca

11. "Overcoming Setbacks Is The Most Desirable Skill For Success", Yvonne LeMar, Ezinearticles.com

Due to space constraints, we have provided a partial list of resources used in writing this book. For a more detailed list, please contact us at media@beinittowinit.com

Everyday is a
Holiday

Every Meal is a
Feast

CPSIA information can be obtained
at www.ICGtesting.com
Printed in the USA
FFOW03n1504080116
20115FF